Disciples of All Nations

Printed in the United States of America

Keen Vision Publishing, LLC

www.publishwithkvp.com

ISBN: 979-8-9927392-6-8

Disciples of All Nations

MAKING THE GREAT COMMISSION OUR DAILY MISSION

KEEN VISION PUBLISHING

Elouise P. Griffith Bradsher, DMin

Table of Contents

INTRODUCTION

Something is missing in the church today. While we gather each Sunday to worship, listen to sermons, and build community, there exists a gap—one that many Christians may not even recognize. The Great Commission calls us to "go and make disciples of all nations," yet too often, we overlook the mission field that lies right in our own neighborhoods. The Gospel is not confined to distant lands or foreign cultures; it is meant to be proclaimed and lived out among us—in our cities, our workplaces, and even within the pews of our churches.

Across the United States, millions of immigrants arrive in search of a better life. Some flee war, poverty, or persecution, while others come seeking education, employment, or to reunite with family. Yet, for many of these individuals, the hope offered by the Gospel remains out of reach. Instead of being embraced by the church, they often find themselves unnoticed, unseen, and unreached. How can a church, built on the foundational mandate to spread the Gospel, fail to extend that message to the very people who live among us? How do we, as a community of believers, miss the opportunity to be a light in the lives of those who need hope the most?

This book is about recognizing and responding to the call that Jesus has placed on every Christian's life. It is a call to break the silence, step out of indifference, and embrace the transformative power of the Gospel in our everyday interactions. Through Scripture, historical insights, and real-life stories, this book challenges, equips, and encourages us to see immigrants as God sees them—not as strangers, but as individuals in dire need of love, belonging, and, most importantly, the message of salvation.

From the very first moments of my own life, the theme of belonging has been woven into my story. I was born in St. Thomas, U.S. Virgin Islands, on September 1, 1961—a decision made by my parents, Thomas and Mary Griffith, who left their homeland of Montserrat in the British West Indies in search of a better future. Their journey was fraught with challenges. As non-U.S. citizens, they had to work tirelessly to secure a place where they could survive and thrive. My father, a trained painter, and my mother, a housekeeper, took on every job available, displaying resilience and determination in the face of uncertainty. My mother was promoted from housekeeper to supervisor at the Bank of Popular, and my father advanced to become an expert painter for the U.S. Virgin Islands Public Works. These successes highlight their contributions as immigrants and their journey to becoming U.S. citizens in 1976.

Growing up, even as a U.S. citizen, I struggled with a sense of not fully belonging. My accent, my customs, and the perspectives I inherited from my immigrant parents set me apart from those around me. When I joined the military just before my twentieth birthday, I encountered even greater challenges. As a Black woman with an immigrant background, I was often overlooked and underestimated despite earning the rank of Senior Non-Commissioned Officer. I had to work twice as hard to prove my worth. Yet, what struck me most was that the same sense of alienation followed me into the church—the very place I expected to find acceptance and belonging.

Instead of experiencing unconditional fellowship, I often felt like an outsider. I witnessed others face similar rejection; one woman I mentored was heartbroken by the superficial warmth offered by fellow believers—warmth that ended at the church doors. At church, she was greeted with smiles and kind words, but outside of Sunday services, no genuine relationships were forged. This disconnect prompted me to search for answers: Why is it that the Church, the body of Christ, struggles to truly embrace those who are different from itself?

As I embarked on my doctoral research at Huntsville Bible College, I was confronted with a single word that kept echoing in my prayers: RECONCILIATION. I came to realize that my own struggles and the struggles of countless others pointed to a deeper issue—a failure on the part of the Church to see immigrants as integral to God's plan. My research revealed that the absence of intentional ministry to immigrants was not merely an oversight but a missed opportunity to fulfill the Great Commission. The revelations of my dissertation compelled me to share this message, and this book is the result of that conviction.

I believe that many churches and Christian leaders do not intentionally neglect immigrants. Often, the problem lies in a lack of awareness and understanding. There is a prevailing assumption that new people will naturally assimilate into the congregation without any deliberate outreach. Others might recognize the need for change but feel unprepared to take action. In some cases, cultural and political rhetoric paints immigrants in a negative light, skewing perceptions away from the truth found in Scripture.

But here is the reality: the nations have come to us. We no longer need to travel overseas to find people from different backgrounds; they are already here, living among us. In His sovereignty, God has placed the Church at a unique crossroads in history—an opportunity to minister to people from every corner of the world right here in our communities. As Romans 12:2 (NIV) reminds us: "Do not conform to the pattern of this world, but be transformed by the renewing of your mind. Then you will be able to test and approve what God's will is—his good, pleasing and perfect will."

It is time for the Church to renew its mindset and recognize that evangelizing to immigrants is not a political issue—it is a Kingdom issue. This is an opportunity for revival, growth, and a renewed commitment to Christ's command.

This book is not just for pastors or church leaders—it is for every Christian. You do not need to be a missionary or an evangelist to fulfill the Great Commission. You simply need to be willing to see people as Jesus sees them and to take deliberate action in your daily life. As you read, I challenge you to reflect, to pray, and to ask God how He might use you to reach those around you. If you are a church leader, consider how your congregation can become more welcoming and intentional about serving immigrant communities. If you are a believer seeking ways to live out your faith more robustly, start by building relationships with those who feel like outsiders.I also encourage you to share what you learn. Talk to your pastors, your fellow church members, and your friends—help them see the opportunities that are right before us. The body of Christ is strongest when it embraces the fullness of God's vision, which includes people from every nation and background.

Throughout history, the Church has thrived when it has embraced its mission to reach all people. When the disciples obeyed Jesus' command, the Gospel spread from Jerusalem to the ends of the earth. When early Christians took risks to share their faith, entire nations were transformed. Today, we stand at a crossroads where we, too, have the opportunity to be part of that transformative legacy. The pressing question is: Will we respond?

My prayer is that as you turn the pages of this book, your heart will be stirred, your vision expanded, and your spirit moved to action. This is not merely about recognizing a problem—it is about stepping into God's plan for His Church. Together, we can fulfill the Great Commission not only in distant lands but right here, in our very communities. This is our mission, and it begins with a renewed commitment to reconciliation and radical love.

I invite you to journey with me through these pages as we explore the themes of hospitality, generosity, love, mercy, and belonging. Each chapter is designed not only to challenge your thinking but also to equip you with practical strategies to transform your ministry and your community. May this book be a catalyst for change—igniting a passion for genuine outreach and a commitment to creating a Church that truly reflects the inclusive love of Christ.

As you reflect on your own experiences of acceptance and rejection, remember that you, too, were once in need of the Church's loving embrace. Let that personal journey fuel your resolve to extend that same grace to others. The path to fulfilling the Great Commission is paved with everyday acts of courage and compassion. And it is through these acts that the Church can become a home away from home—a place where every soul finds refuge and every heart experiences the transformative power of God's love.

Embrace this call with open arms and a willing spirit. The challenge before us is great, but so is the promise of God's abundant grace. As you commit to stepping out in faith, know that you are not alone—God's Spirit is with you, guiding and empowering you every step of the way.

This is our mission. This is our time. And it all begins with you.

Chapter One

THE COMMAND TO TRANSCEND BORDERS

The Great Commission is more than a directive; it is a mission that shapes the identity of every believer. When Jesus commanded His disciples to go and make disciples of all nations, He wasn't just speaking to those standing before Him—He was speaking to us, the Church today. This is not an optional task but a foundational part of our faith. Yet, despite its significance, many Christians struggle to apply this calling in their everyday lives, especially when it comes to reaching those who are different from them—immigrants, foreigners, and those on the fringes of society.

Imagine standing on the shores of the Sea of Galilee, with the gentle lapping of water and a palpable sense of anticipation in the air. In that moment, Jesus's words resonated with a power transcending time and space. His declaration in Matthew 28:18-20 NIV— "All authority in heaven and on earth has been given to me. Therefore, go and make disciples of all nations, baptizing them in the name of the Father and of the Son and of the Holy

Spirit, and teaching them to obey everything I have commanded you. And surely I am with you always, to the very end of the age." —was not just a farewell address; it was a mandate for action. The disciples, filled with both awe and uncertainty, were called to step beyond what was comfortable and familiar. They were challenged to cross boundaries—physical, cultural, and spiritual—in order to spread the message of salvation. This command is possibly more relevant today than it was then! It challenges us to look beyond our fears and prejudices and reach out to those who are often overlooked by our society.

THE HEART OF THE GREAT COMMISSION

To truly grasp the essence of this command, we must first understand what it means to "transcend borders." The phrase "all nations" is radical—it shatters the notion of exclusivity. Jesus was not calling for a limited ministry confined by cultural, ethnic, or national boundaries. Instead, He envisioned a church that reaches every corner of humanity. In a time when divisions were deeply ingrained in society, this was revolutionary. Today, these divisions persist in various forms, and the Church must constantly examine itself to ensure that it does not inadvertently replicate the very barriers it is called to break down.

Think back to a moment in your own life when you encountered someone who was entirely different from you—a person whose language, customs, or appearance set them apart. How did that encounter make you feel? Now, imagine if that difference became a reason to withhold kindness. The Great Commission challenges us to rise above such instincts, to see every individual as a beloved creation of God, worthy of our attention and care. It is not merely about missionary work in far-off lands; it's about transforming our own communities by embracing those who are different.

THE CHALLENGE OF OBEDIENCE

The early Church's journey provides a compelling model of what it means to obey this command. For the disciples, the call to "make disciples of all nations" was fraught with challenges. They were a group of individuals who had known Jesus intimately, yet when faced with the task of reaching beyond their familiar circle, they experienced fear and uncertainty. Peter's transformative vision in Acts 10 is a striking example. Confronted by a vision in which God declared that the Gospel was not limited to the Jews, Peter's heart was changed forever. His encounter with Cornelius—a Roman centurion—opened his eyes to the reality that God's grace extends to all people, regardless of their ethnic background.

Similarly, the Apostle Paul's life is a testament to radical obedience. Paul traversed the Roman Empire, enduring hardships, imprisonments, and even shipwrecks, all because he refused to limit the reach of the Gospel. His epistles speak not only of theological depth but also of the immense cost of discipleship. Paul's unwavering commitment challenges us today: are we prepared to step outside our comfort zones to engage with those who are vastly different from us, even if it means facing our own fears and uncertainties?

The stories of Peter and Paul remind us that obeying the Great Commission requires courage—a willingness to venture into the unknown and trust in God's promise of presence and power. Their journeys are not merely historical accounts; they are blueprints for every believer who longs to see the Gospel thrive in a world that is often divided and fearful.

THE GREAT COMMISSION IN OUR COMMUNITIES

For many, mission work is synonymous with traveling to distant lands. Yet, the reality is that God has placed people from every nation right in our own neighborhoods. Immigration has brought millions of individuals from diverse cultural backgrounds into the heart of our communities. Despite their significant contributions, many immigrants remain unreached by the Gospel. They live among us, often facing immense challenges, yet the Church frequently overlooks them.

It is easy to say that the message of the Gospel is universal, but the practical outworking of this truth is far more challenging. Many Christians hesitate to engage with immigrants due to fear, misunderstanding, or simply not knowing where to begin. Some believe that effective evangelism requires extensive theological training or specific skill sets, while others allow cultural and political narratives to distort their perception of immigrants. However, the Great Commission calls us to shift our perspective. Instead of viewing cultural differences as obstacles, we are to see them as opportunities—opportunities to expand God's kingdom, to build bridges of understanding, and to share the love of Christ in every encounter.

Imagine a community where every interaction becomes a chance to witness the love of God. Whether it is welcoming a refugee family, mentoring an international student, or simply sharing a meal with an immigrant coworker, each act of genuine kindness serves as a small but significant step toward fulfilling the

Great Commission. The Church is uniquely positioned to be the catalyst for such change, yet it must first recognize and embrace the call to transcend borders—both literally and figuratively.

BREAKING DOWN BARRIERS

One of the greatest challenges to fulfilling the Great Commission is the presence of invisible barriers that separate us from those who are different. Many immigrants face struggles that are often overlooked by those who have lived in the same country their entire lives. Language barriers, financial difficulties, and social isolation are common realities for those trying to adjust to a new environment. The Church has a unique opportunity to meet these needs—not just through words but through tangible acts of love and service.

Consider the parable of the Good Samaritan, where Jesus teaches that true neighborliness transcends cultural, social, and ethnic boundaries. The Samaritan did not hesitate to help a stranger in need; he saw beyond differences to the heart of the person suffering. If we are truly following Christ, we must be willing to do the same—breaking down barriers, offering practical help, and creating an environment where every individual feels valued.

Each barrier broken is a step toward a more inclusive Church—one that reflects the radical love of Jesus. When we open our hearts and minds, we begin to see that the same God who called the disciples to reach "all nations" is calling us to reach those who stand before us every day.

PRACTICAL STEPS TO ENGAGE IN THE GREAT COMMISSION

Understanding the Great Commission is one thing, but putting it into practice is another. Many believers desire to obey Christ's command, yet they often struggle with how to begin. Here are some practical ways to engage in this mission:

- **Develop Relationships:** Take time to build genuine friendships with people from diverse backgrounds. Ask questions, learn about their culture, and show sincere interest in their lives. These personal connections form the foundation of effective evangelism.

- **Be Hospitable:** Open your home and share meals with those who may feel like outsiders. Hospitality is one of the simplest yet most impactful ways to reflect Christ's love and break down barriers of isolation.

- **Get Involved in Local Ministries:** Many churches and community organizations have programs that serve immigrants and refugees. Find ways to volunteer your time and resources. Engaging with these initiatives not only meets immediate needs but also creates opportunities for deeper spiritual conversations.

- **Share Your Faith Naturally:** Evangelism is not confined to street preaching or formal events. Often, it is about everyday conversations—sharing how Christ has transformed your life and being a living testimony to His love. Allow your faith to shine through in simple, authentic interactions.

- **Pray for Open Doors:** Consistently ask God to provide

opportunities to share His love with people from all nations. Pray for boldness, wisdom, and sensitivity in every interaction. A prayerful heart is a powerful tool in breaking down barriers.

Each of these steps is designed to be practical and relational, moving beyond theoretical knowledge into actionable ministry. As you consider these approaches, remember that even the smallest act of genuine kindness can have a profound impact on someone's life.

A CALL TO ACTION

The Great Commission is not just for pastors, missionaries, or evangelists—it's for every believer. Jesus didn't say, "If you feel like it, go and make disciples." He said, "Go." The call is clear, and the time is now.

Ask yourself: Are you truly living in obedience to this command? Are there people in your life who desperately need to hear about Jesus? Are there immigrants or refugees in your community whom you could welcome and minister to? This chapter is not merely about understanding the Great Commission; it's about responding to it with boldness and compassion.

As you reflect on the message of the Great Commission, consider that the nations have already come to us. The very streets you walk, the neighborhoods you live in, and the congregations you attend are teeming with people from every corner of the globe. They carry with them stories of struggle, hope, and resilience—stories that echo the ancient narrative of redemption. It is our responsibility to not only acknowledge their presence but to actively reach out, build relationships, and make disciples as Jesus commanded. Take a moment to examine your own life and ministry. What steps are you taking to transcend cultural and social barriers? How are you ensuring that the love of Christ is evident in every interaction? This is a call to action—a plea to step out in faith, break down walls, and create a community where every person feels welcomed, valued, and loved.

The Church's mission is not an abstract ideal; it is a tangible, daily pursuit. Every time you extend a warm greeting to a stranger, every time you share a meal, and every time you engage in heartfelt conversation, you are fulfilling the call to make disciples of all nations. Your actions, no matter how small, have the power to transform lives and build bridges that lead to lasting relationships.

Let us be a Church that embodies the radical love of Jesus—a Church that sees beyond differences and embraces every individual as a beloved child of God. In doing so, we not only honor the Great Commission but also create a legacy of unity and hope. May your life, your ministry, and your community be defined by a bold commitment to break down barriers and build bridges of compassion.

The time for action is now. Stand up, reach out, and let the transformative power of the Gospel guide your every step. In your willingness to serve, you reflect the heart of our Savior, who came not to condemn but to redeem. Let your ministry be a living testimony to the truth that, in God's eyes, every person matters. Embrace the challenge, and together, let us expand God's kingdom right where we are.

Chapter Two

BRIDGING CULTURES WITH COMPASSION

The presence of immigrants in the United States has been met with a mixture of responses from society—and the Church is no exception. While some congregations have embraced immigrants with open arms, others have remained indifferent, and some have even contributed to exclusionary rhetoric. This reality raises a sobering question: How well is the Church fulfilling Christ's command to love and welcome the stranger?

The Great Commission extends beyond geographical borders. It is not simply a call to send missionaries to foreign lands but a mandate to make disciples among all people—including those who now live among us. Immigration remains one of the most polarizing issues in the U.S., entangled with politics, economics, and cultural identity. Yet, the Church is called to rise above these societal debates and respond with genuine, Christ-like compassion. The challenge is clear: Are we truly seeing and serving immigrants as Christ would?

GOD'S LAW OVER MAN'S LAW

Throughout history, human laws have often contradicted God's call to justice, mercy, and love. Nations have erected barriers, denied refuge, and enacted policies that dehumanize the vulnerable. As believers, however, our response to immigration must not be dictated solely by government regulations or societal fears. Scripture reminds us that our ultimate allegiance is to God's law—a law that consistently commands us to embrace and protect the foreigner.

The Bible is replete with directives on how God's people should treat immigrants. From the Old Testament to the teachings of Jesus, we are instructed to extend love, kindness, and justice to the stranger. Leviticus 19:34 states: "The foreigner residing among you must be treated as your native-born. Love them as yourself, for you were foreigners in Egypt. I am the Lord your God."

Likewise, Deuteronomy 10:18-19 declares: "He defends the cause of the fatherless and the widow, and loves the foreigner residing among you, giving them food and clothing. And you are to love those who are foreigners, for you yourselves were foreigners in Egypt."

In Matthew 25:35-40, Jesus personalizes this command: "For I was hungry and you gave me something to eat, I was thirsty and you gave me something to drink, I was a stranger and you invited me in... Truly I tell you, whatever you did for one of the least of these brothers and sisters of mine, you did for me."

If we claim to follow Christ, our treatment of immigrants must align with His example. The Church must not let legal or political arguments overshadow the foundational command to love our neighbor. When we welcome the immigrant, we are, in effect, welcoming Christ Himself. This mandate is not a political act but a spiritual calling that reflects the essence of God's love.

Jesus Himself ministered to those considered outsiders— Samaritans, Gentiles, and even Roman officials. He looked beyond legal status and cultural labels, seeing only souls in desperate need of grace. The same heart must beat in the modern Church as we heed the biblical call to love the foreigner and break down the barriers that separate us.

It is essential to internalize that God's law supersedes man's law. When we see immigration issues through God's lens, we are compelled to act justly and compassionately, regardless of prevailing political opinions or societal pressures. This perspective should transform our approach to ministry, making every outreach a reflection of divine love.

A BIBLICAL PERSPECTIVE ON MIGRATION

Migration is not a modern phenomenon; it has been integral to God's plan since the dawn of time. The movement of people across lands is woven into the very fabric of the biblical narrative. Abraham's departure from his homeland in obedience to God is a seminal example. He left behind familiar territory to step into the unknown, trusting in God's promise. Similarly, Joseph, taken to Egypt under duress, rose to a position where God used him to save many lives. In the book of Ruth, we see a Moabite woman welcomed into Israel and honored for her loyalty—a testament to the transformative power of inclusion. Even Jesus, whose early childhood was marked by His family's flight to Egypt to escape

King Herod's threat (Matthew 2:13-15), embodies the refugee experience.

These narratives illustrate that migration has always been part of God's redemptive plan. They remind us that God is at work in every movement of people. The current wave of immigration is not a deviation from His plan; it is a continuation. The Church must ask itself: Is God using this migration to bring people closer to Him? Instead of resisting change, the Church should seize this opportunity to minister and share the Gospel.

Our neighborhoods are not barren or homogeneous—they are vibrant mosaics of cultures and languages. The nations are no longer far away; they are right here at our doorstep. Just as God used migration in ancient times to bring about His purposes, He is using it today to expand His kingdom. Jesus' ministry itself was a series of encounters with people from various backgrounds—whether it was the Samaritan woman at the well (John 4) or the Roman centurion whose faith He commended (Matthew 8:5-13). Each encounter is a reminder that the Gospel breaks down cultural and societal boundaries, inviting us to embrace diversity with open hearts.

As we ponder the biblical perspective on migration, it becomes clear that God's plan is not about preserving exclusivity but about expanding inclusivity. This realization should compel the Church to view every immigrant as an opportunity to share in the redemptive story of Christ—a story that unites all nations and peoples under one banner.

THE INTERSECTION OF FAITH AND POLITICS

In today's polarized environment, discussions about immigration are often deeply entangled with politics. Many believers struggle to reconcile their faith with their political stance on immigration policies. Yet, Jesus never instructed His followers to align with any political ideology; He called us to align with the Kingdom of God.

Historically, the United States has had a complicated relationship with immigration. The Chinese Exclusion Act of 1882, the restrictive quotas imposed in the 1920s, and the internment of Japanese Americans during World War II are stark examples of how fear and prejudice have shaped policies. More recently, debates over border security, asylum seekers, and refugee admissions continue to divide communities—both politically and religiously.

Rather than allowing these debates to paralyze us, the Church must return to the foundational truth that every person is made in God's image and is worthy of love, dignity, and care. The Church should speak out against laws and policies that dehumanize and marginalize the vulnerable. Our mission is to advocate for compassionate solutions that honor justice and mercy—values that are intrinsic to our faith.

When we put politics aside and focus on our identity as disciples of Christ, we begin to see immigrants not as political problems, but as people in need of our help. Our faith must guide us to stand in the gap, challenge the status quo, and embody a love that transcends partisan divides. In doing so, we create a powerful testimony of God's grace—one that speaks louder than any political rhetoric. As we reflect on these issues, let us recognize that the Church is uniquely positioned to offer an alternative vision—one where compassion, understanding, and mercy prevail over division and fear. The time has come for us to move beyond political debates and let our faith be the guiding light that shapes our response to immigration.

PRACTICAL STEPS FOR THE CHURCH

Creating a welcoming church requires intentionality and a willingness to act. It is not enough to claim that all are welcome; the Church must implement practical steps to ensure immigrants feel seen, valued, and fully integrated into the community. Here are some actionable strategies:

1. **Preach Biblical Hospitality:** Regularly incorporate messages about God's heart for immigrants into sermons, Bible studies, and small groups. When congregants hear the consistent call to welcome the stranger, fear-based narratives can be dismantled. Teaching hospitality should be rooted in Scripture—illustrating how the Church is called to mirror the boundless love of God.

2. **Create Support Systems:** Immigrants often face challenges like language barriers, employment difficulties, and cultural dislocation. Offering practical support such as ESL classes, job training sessions, and mentorship programs can make a significant difference. These programs empower individuals and provide them with tools to thrive in their new environment, demonstrating the Church's commitment to holistic care.

3. **Celebrate Cultural Diversity:** A truly welcoming Church

is one that embraces the richness of diversity. Incorporate different languages into worship services, acknowledge and celebrate various cultural holidays, and invite immigrant members to share their testimonies. This not only fosters a sense of belonging but also enriches the entire community by showcasing the myriad ways God's love is expressed.

4. **Engage in Advocacy:** Beyond the walls of the Church, it is essential to speak up for those who are marginalized. Partner with organizations that offer legal aid and support and advocate for fair, humane immigration policies. By taking a stand for justice, the Church becomes a prophetic voice in society—one that champions the rights and dignity of every individual.

5. **Develop a Welcoming Ministry:** Establish a dedicated team tasked with reaching out to immigrants. This ministry can create welcome packets that include essential information about the Church, provide interpreters for non-native speakers, and conduct personal follow-ups to ensure that newcomers feel truly integrated. Such initiatives build a personal, relational bridge that welcomes immigrants not just as visitors but as valued members of the Church family.

These practical steps are not isolated programs; they are expressions of a holistic vision where the Church actively embodies the love of Christ. When implemented thoughtfully, these initiatives transform the Church into a sanctuary that reflects the unity and diversity of God's kingdom.

A CALL TO ACTION

The challenge before the Church is clear: Will we stand by while immigrants remain on the margins, or will we actively embody the love of Christ by welcoming them into our spiritual family? This chapter has shown that welcoming immigrants is not an optional extra–it is central to our mission as disciples of Christ. The Great Commission calls us to make disciples of all nations, and that includes those who live among us. Biblical narratives remind us that migration is part of God's grand design, and the early Church demonstrated that when cultural barriers are broken down, the Gospel flourishes.

Now is the time for action. I urge you, whether you are a church leader or a committed believer, to take these insights to heart and put them into practice. Evaluate your current ministry: Are you creating spaces where immigrants feel genuinely welcome? If not, consider how you might integrate the practical steps outlined above. Begin with small acts of intentional hospitality and gradually build programs that transform your Church into a true home for all.

Ask yourself: How does my personal approach reflect the radical love of Christ? What concrete steps can I take to break down barriers in my community? Your willingness to act is not only a reflection of your faith–it is a powerful testimony to the transformative power of the Gospel.

Every act of kindness, every meal shared, every word of encouragement is a step toward fulfilling the Great Commission. As you reach out to someone different from you, remember that you are extending the hand of Christ. Your actions can create ripples of change that extend far beyond your immediate circle, impacting entire communities and, ultimately, nations.

I challenge you to see the immigrant not as a problem to be managed but as a beloved child of God—a person with a story, a past, and a future that is intertwined with the divine narrative. Let your ministry be characterized by a relentless commitment to love, break down barriers, and create a community where everyone, regardless of background, feels at home.

Embrace the call to make disciples of all nations with courage and conviction. Stand up, step out, and let your life be a beacon of hope and inclusion. The Church has a pivotal role in shaping a future where every individual is welcomed, where the love of Christ is evident in every interaction, and where the Great Commission is lived out in practical, transformative ways.

May your journey be marked by bold, compassionate action, and may your ministry reflect the limitless love of our Savior. The time is now—fulfill your calling and help create a Church that truly embodies the heart of God.

Thoughts

Chapter Three

RADICAL HOSPITALITY

R adical hospitality is not just an act of kindness; it is a defining hallmark of the Church's mission. It reflects God's limitless love and acceptance, calling believers to engage deeply with the marginalized—including immigrants— within society. True hospitality goes far beyond merely opening the doors of a building. It is about embracing people into the body of Christ, meeting their needs, and walking alongside them on their journey of faith. In a world where many feel isolated and unwelcome, the call to practice radical hospitality is more urgent than ever.

The need for radical hospitality has never been more pressing. Across the nation, churches find themselves at a crossroads. Cultural shifts, political tensions, and social divisions have all impacted how ministries engage with immigrants and other marginalized groups. Sadly, many congregations have remained hesitant or even indifferent. Yet, Jesus never modeled indifference—He modeled radical, sacrificial love. In His life,

Jesus broke down barriers, welcomed outcasts, and transformed lives through His embrace of those deemed different by society.

This chapter delves into the nuances of radical hospitality, guided by scriptural precedence and the teachings of Jesus Christ. It challenges the Church to embody these principles and foster genuine inclusivity, bridging the gap between immigrants and native believers in a way that honors God. Churches must reassess how they conduct ministry—both within their walls and in the broader community—to ensure that every individual is met with compassion, dignity, and grace.

Imagine walking into a room full of strangers, feeling the weight of eyes upon you, uncertain whether you belong. Now, picture being met with warmth and open arms—someone who goes the extra mile to ensure you feel comfortable, valued, and understood. This is the essence of radical hospitality: a grace-filled embrace that goes far beyond superficial courtesy to forge genuine connections.

UNDERSTANDING RADICAL HOSPITALITY

Radical hospitality is characterized by five key themes: generosity, love at work, mercy, hospitality, and community. These themes intersect to create a practice that is not merely about politeness but about transformational encounters. The Church is called to be a living testament to these principles, extending a hand to those who find themselves isolated or marginalized.

Scripture provides numerous examples of this ethos. Consider Abraham's encounter with divine visitors in Genesis 18:1-8. Abraham welcomed three strangers into his home with such generosity and care—without knowing they were angels—

that his actions became a timeless model for hospitality. Similarly, the laws in Leviticus 19:33-34 command the Israelites to love strangers as they love themselves, urging them to remember that they were once foreigners in Egypt. These biblical directives compel us to view hospitality not as an optional nicety but as a sacred duty.

The call to radical hospitality is not confined to the Old Testament. The New Testament continually reinforces this theme, demonstrating that God's heart is for the marginalized and that true community is built on inclusion and love.

OLD TESTAMENT EXAMPLES OF HOSPITALITY

Consider standing at a crossroads in a vast desert—hungry, thirsty, and in desperate need of shelter. Abraham's willingness to offer rest and sustenance to three divine visitors in such a barren setting epitomizes the heart of biblical hospitality. His actions remind us that in every encounter, we have the opportunity to welcome the unknown and to prioritize the needs of others over our own comfort.

The narrative of Abraham's encounter is more than an isolated incident; it sets a precedent for how we are to treat strangers. By extending care and honor to those who come into our lives, we open ourselves to divine blessings that often exceed our expectations. Moreover, Leviticus 19:33-34 further cements this ethic, instructing the Israelites to treat the foreigner as a native, to love them as they love themselves. This command is rooted in empathy and in the recognition that every person carries the image of God, regardless of their origins. Such Old Testament examples serve as foundational blueprints for radical hospitality.

They not only instruct us on what is expected but also inspire us to act with boldness and compassion.

NEW TESTAMENT TEACHINGS ON HOSPITALITY

The New Testament amplifies the call to radical hospitality through parables and the life of Jesus. Picture being told the story of the Good Samaritan—a man who defies cultural boundaries to aid a wounded stranger. In Luke 10:25-37, the Samaritan's actions challenge the prevailing prejudices of His time. Here, Jesus doesn't just tell us to be kind; He calls us to be transformative, to show love that cuts through the divisions of race, class, and nationality.

Similarly, the teaching in Matthew 25:35-40, where Jesus explains that serving the least among us is equivalent to serving Him, provides a powerful incentive for radical hospitality. When we serve others, we are serving Christ Himself. This message is reinforced time and again in the New Testament, urging believers to put aside societal barriers and to engage with others with genuine compassion and care.

These teachings culminate in a vision of the Church as a community marked by radical love and inclusivity—a community where every act of kindness is a step toward breaking down the walls that separate us.

JESUS AS THE MODEL OF HOSPITALITY

Jesus' ministry offers the ultimate example of radical hospitality. His life was a series of encounters with those who were often shunned by society. Whether it was dining with Zacchaeus, a tax collector despised by many (Luke 19:1-10), or engaging in conversation with the Samaritan woman at the well (John 4:7-30), Jesus consistently broke social norms to demonstrate God's love.

In John 13:1-17, when Jesus washed His disciples' feet, He not only performed a humble act of service but also redefined what it meant to be a leader. True hospitality, as Jesus modeled, involves humility, selflessness, and a willingness to serve others, regardless of their status. His actions show us that radical hospitality is not about grand gestures alone—it is about the every day, sacrificial acts that build genuine relationships.

Jesus' example challenges us to reconsider how we engage with those around us. If the Savior of the world could see beyond cultural and social boundaries, then surely we are called to do the same. His life is a powerful testimony to the transformative nature of hospitality, urging us to open our hearts to all, especially to those who are most in need.

A CALL TO ACTION

The mission is urgent. The nations are at our doorstep. Every act of kindness, every gesture of welcome, every time you open your heart and home, you fulfill a part of the Great Commission. Remember that the Church is not merely a building—it is a living, breathing community where love is practiced and barriers are dismantled. Your commitment to radical hospitality can transform lives and communities, leaving a lasting legacy of inclusion and compassion.

Let us not remain complacent. Instead, let our actions speak of the Gospel's transformative power. Step out in faith, take risks, and embrace the call to make our Church a true home away from home. Let every conversation, every shared meal, and every act of kindness be a declaration of God's unending love—a love that transcends all boundaries and unites us as one body in Christ.

As you reflect on the words of this chapter, I invite you to commit to a journey of radical hospitality. The task is not easy, but the reward is eternal. Your willingness to reach out, to welcome, and to build bridges of understanding is a powerful testimony to the transformative power of the Gospel. Let your life be a beacon of hope—a living example of what it means to be a Church that truly embodies the heart of Christ.

May your actions inspire others to join you in creating a community where every person is embraced as a beloved child of God. This is our calling. This is our mission. And it begins with each one of us opening our hearts to the radical, inclusive, and boundless love that God has shown us.

Chapter Four

A CHEERFUL GIVER

Picture a world where every interaction begins with kindness, and each encounter brims with hope and empathy. Such a world may seem idealistic, yet through acts of generosity, we step closer to realizing that vision. The call to be generous is not merely a suggestion; it is an invitation to partake in the transformative power of grace—a grace that mirrors the heart of Christ, who gives unconditionally. As we delve into this chapter, I invite you to reflect on how generosity changes not only those who receive but also those who give. How might we, as individuals and as a community of believers, live out this sacred call in tangible, transformative ways?

Generosity stands as one of the most profound expressions of Christian faith. It mirrors the boundless love and compassion demonstrated by Jesus Christ and reflects a spirit that transcends social and cultural boundaries. Just as God created mankind in His own image, as stated in Genesis 1:27, generosity is woven into the very fabric of creation. This divine characteristic calls us to move beyond mere transactional interactions and to embody a spirit of giving that mirrors God's own generosity. In a nation like the United States–where the contributions and challenges of immigrants are deeply interwoven with society's narrative–Christians have a unique opportunity to emulate Jesus's example of generosity. In doing so, we fulfill the Great Commission: to make disciples of all nations.

Before we journey deeper into the concept of generosity, I invite you to pause and reflect on your own experiences. Think of a time when someone's unexpected kindness brightened your day, or when your own act of giving left you feeling more connected and alive. That moment, that feeling, is at the core of radical generosity–a spirit that transforms both the giver and the receiver.

UNDERSTANDING JESUS'S GENEROSITY

Think about a time when generosity surprised you–an unexpected kindness from a stranger or a profound act of compassion that altered your perspective. Such moments often leave an indelible mark on our hearts, challenging us to expand our capacity for giving. As we explore the life of Jesus, we discover countless examples of radical generosity that compel us to reflect on our own lives. Jesus's actions challenge us to move beyond our comfort zones, embrace a lifestyle of sacrificial giving, and let His generosity shape every interaction.

The life of Jesus Christ is arguably the most profound example of generosity the world has ever witnessed. His teachings and His actions set a standard for how Christians are called to live–engaging the world with open hearts, willing hands, and receptive minds. Jesus's example challenges us to reflect on our own lives and to align our actions with His. The call to generosity beckons us to embody the love of Christ, reminding us that we, too, are capable of extraordinary acts of giving because Jesus demonstrated them first.

Jesus's generosity was not sporadic or incidental; it was an integral part of His ministry. In Matthew 14:13-21, when Jesus fed the five thousand, He illustrated that His concern extended not just to spiritual hunger but also to physical needs. Through this miracle, He revealed a profound compassion for humanity, urging us to meet the multifaceted needs of those around us. In Mark 10:46-52, Jesus heals the blind man Bartimaeus, showing that no request is too small and that every individual, no matter how seemingly insignificant, is worthy of His compassionate attention. These acts remind us that true generosity encompasses not only material wealth but also the gift of time, presence, and empathy—the very qualities that Jesus exemplified in every encounter.

Moreover, Jesus extended His generosity through radical inclusivity, welcoming those whom society often rejected. His encounter with the Samaritan woman at the well, as recounted in John 4:1-26, defied the cultural norms of His time by erasing the boundaries of race and custom. In honoring her humanity, Jesus extended an invitation not only to faith but to be seen and valued. This was a profound act of generosity—one that calls us to cross divides and extend grace to all. Similarly, in Matthew 8:5-13, Jesus's response to the Roman centurion demonstrated His willingness to reach across ethnic and political lines. By acknowledging the centurion's faith and healing his servant,

Jesus revealed that divine generosity transcends human divisions, affirming that every person is deserving of His compassion.

These biblical narratives serve as a blueprint for us. They call us to recognize the inherent dignity in every human encounter, to examine our lives, and to ask ourselves how we might more fully reflect His example. Let Jesus's life inspire us to expand our own capacity for kindness and sacrifice, transforming our interactions into acts of radical generosity.

THE GREAT COMMISSION AND GENEROSITY

The Great Commission is not merely a directive to spread the Gospel—it is a call to manifest the inclusive and generous love that Jesus lived and taught. In Matthew 28:19-20, when Jesus commands His disciples to "make disciples of all nations," He establishes a foundation of inclusivity that challenges us to transcend our own circles and cultural boundaries. Generosity, then, becomes a cornerstone of this mission. It acts as a bridge that connects diverse communities and opens hearts to the transforming message of the Gospel.

When we view evangelism through the lens of generosity, we begin to see that it is not solely about preaching the Word. It is about opening our hearts, sharing our resources, and building relationships that overcome social barriers. Generosity serves as a catalyst—it breaks down walls of mistrust and fear and creates opportunities for the Gospel to take root in lives that have long felt abandoned or forgotten.

Moreover, when churches extend generosity to immigrant communities, they shift outreach from a mere duty to a vibrant, relational ministry. Immigrants, often seen only as recipients of aid, are instead welcomed as active participants in God's mission. This redefinition transforms generosity from a transactional act into a dynamic process of relational discipleship, enriching both the giver and the receiver. In doing so, believers reflect the vision of God's kingdom—a community where every individual contributes to the collective strength and purpose of the Church.

I invite you to ask: How does my generosity open doors for others? How can my acts of giving serve as a powerful testimony to the transformative power of the Gospel? Let these questions guide you as you live out the Great Commission with a heart dedicated to generosity.

GENEROSITY AS EVANGELISM

Generosity is intricately woven into the fabric of evangelism. It provides a practical avenue through which the spirit of Christ is made tangible in everyday life. When we engage in acts of generosity, we build trust and create an atmosphere where divine truths can be shared naturally. This approach to evangelism goes beyond words or doctrinal debates—it is a living demonstration of Christ's love and abundance.

When churches meet the physical needs of immigrant communities—whether by feeding the hungry, providing shelter, or offering medical care—they create a foundation upon which deeper spiritual conversations can take root. These acts of giving, reminiscent of Jesus feeding the multitude or healing the afflicted, serve as compelling testimonies of the Gospel. When we address the challenges faced by immigrants, such as food insecurity or language barriers, we build bridges of understanding that enable the seeds of faith to flourish.

Generosity, when integrated into evangelism, transforms fleeting encounters into lasting relationships. It invites both the giver and the receiver into a dynamic exchange where the love of Christ becomes evident in every interaction. Each act of kindness sends ripples throughout the community, gradually breaking down long-held barriers and opening hearts to the truth of the Gospel. In this way, generosity is not just a means of providing aid—it is a strategy for sharing the hope and renewal that is found in Jesus.

Reflect on those moments in your own life when an unexpected act of kindness led to a deeper understanding or a new relationship. These instances are part of a larger tapestry of generosity that, when woven together, creates a solid foundation for evangelistic outreach.

PRACTICAL EXPRESSIONS OF GENEROSITY

The practical outworking of generosity is essential for transforming communities and advancing the Great Commission. These expressions of generosity are not mere gestures; they are deliberate, tangible actions that reflect the love and compassion of Christ. Consider how your community might reflect God's abundance through concrete initiatives:

1. **Food Pantries and Clothing Drives:** Establishing food banks, clothing closets, and shelter programs addresses immediate needs. Such initiatives echo the miracle of Jesus feeding the multitudes, reminding us that physical nourishment is a vital expression of His love.

2. **Language and Education Support:** Many immigrants face

significant challenges due to language barriers. Offering ESL classes, tutoring programs, and educational workshops equips immigrants with the skills needed to succeed, empowering them to thrive in their new environment.

3. **Legal Assistance and Advocacy:** Partner with organizations that offer legal aid to help immigrants navigate complex legal systems. Advocating for fair and compassionate immigration policies demonstrates the Church's commitment to justice and mercy.

4. **Intercultural Celebrations:** Host events that celebrate the rich cultural diversity within your community—multicultural festivals, heritage nights, or language exchange programs can create opportunities for meaningful interactions and foster a sense of belonging.

5. **Mentorship and Counseling Programs:** Develop programs that pair immigrant families with experienced members of the congregation who can offer guidance, support, and friendship. Counseling services, both spiritual and practical, address the emotional and psychological challenges that often accompany migration.

6. **Volunteer Networks:** Form dedicated volunteer groups to assist immigrants with practical needs such as transportation, childcare, or financial literacy. These networks extend the Church's care beyond its walls, building a community of support that uplifts and empowers.

Each of these initiatives serves as a practical manifestation of generosity, transforming the Church into a sanctuary where every individual feels valued and supported. By investing in these tangible expressions of generosity, churches not only meet immediate needs but also lay the groundwork for long-term relationships and discipleship.

INTERNAL TRANSFORMATION AND GENEROSITY

For the Church to truly embody the generosity of Christ, there must first be an internal transformation—a change of heart that radiates outward in every interaction. This process of internal transformation is essential; it sets the tone for how we engage with the world.

Cultural awareness and sensitivity play crucial roles in this transformation. As the Church strives to understand the diverse backgrounds of immigrants, it must engage in ongoing education and self-reflection. Workshops, training sessions, and facilitated dialogues can help congregants identify and overcome their own biases, enabling them to interact with others in a more empathetic and respectful manner.

This internal transformation goes beyond mere intellectual understanding; it is about changing hearts. When church members begin to see immigrants as fellow bearers of God's image, their willingness to give—and to receive—grows naturally. Personal stories of transformation, shared within the community, serve as powerful reminders of how acts of generosity can change lives. Reflect on your own journey: How has a single act of kindness or a generous gesture altered your perspective? These experiences are the seeds of internal change that, when nurtured, can lead to a broader culture of generosity within the Church.

As each individual undergoes this inward transformation, it

radiates outward, creating a Church that not only serves others but also embodies the true spirit of the Gospel. This personal growth is the foundation upon which a unified and compassionate community is built—a community where every act of generosity is a testament to the transforming power of God's love.

A CALL TO ACTION

The call to be a cheerful giver is not merely a personal challenge—it is a divine mandate that fuels the Great Commission. Now, as we conclude this chapter on generosity, the time to act is unequivocal.

I challenge you, as a leader and as a believer, to examine your life and your ministry with fresh eyes. Ask yourself: Are you living out the call to be a cheerful giver? Is your Church actively engaging with immigrant communities through tangible, transformative acts of generosity? Consider how you can implement the practical strategies discussed in this chapter. Whether it's establishing food pantries, hosting intercultural events, offering language and educational support, or forming dedicated volunteer networks, every initiative is an opportunity to embody the generous heart of Christ.

Your commitment to living generously is not just an expression of faith; it is a powerful declaration of the Gospel. Every time you extend a helping hand, every time you share your resources, you reflect the unending love of God. Your actions become a beacon of hope—a testimony to the transformative power of generosity that reaches far beyond the confines of your Church.

Remember, the Great Commission calls us to make disciples of all nations, and that mission begins at home. The Church is not merely a building; it is a living community where every member is invited to participate in the Kingdom of God. By embracing radical generosity, you create an environment where immigrants feel welcomed, where barriers are broken down, and where the love of Christ is evident in every interaction.

I urge you to step out in faith. Let the example of Jesus—who fed the multitudes, healed the sick, and embraced those considered unworthy—guide your actions. Embrace the challenge of being a cheerful giver, and let your life and ministry serve as a catalyst for change. The opportunity to transform lives is at your fingertips, and it begins with one act of generosity, one act of love, and one open-hearted step forward.

The time for action is now. As you lead your community, let every decision and every act of kindness be a reflection of God's boundless grace. Your commitment to generosity can and will transform not only your own life but also the lives of countless others. Embrace this call with courage and conviction, knowing that each step you take is a step toward fulfilling the Great Commission and building God's kingdom on earth.

May your ministry be defined by a relentless commitment to generosity—a generosity that transforms hearts, unites communities, and lights the way for others to follow. Let your Church be a sanctuary where every person, regardless of background, finds a home. In doing so, you not only honor the legacy of Christ's love but also create a future where every act of giving becomes a testament to the power of the Gospel.

Step out, be bold, and let your life be a living example of cheerful giving. This is your moment to shine as a beacon of hope and to make a lasting impact on the world around you.

Chapter Five

NOTHING WITHOUT LOVE

Consider the last time you witnessed the power of love in action—perhaps a simple act of kindness that brought unexpected joy or a compassionate gesture that offered solace during a difficult time. For pastors and church leaders, these moments are the heartbeat of ministry. Love transforms lives, heals wounds, and builds bridges where division once reigned. It is the silent force that drives our mission, turning theory into reality and igniting change in communities. This chapter delves into how love is not only essential to the Great Commission but is also the catalyst for profound ministry. It challenges us to review ourselves, reimagine our outreach, and fully integrate the radical theme of "love at work" into every facet of our ministry.

LOVE IN THE GREAT COMMISSION

Imagine embarking on the mission set out in Matthew 28:19-20, equipped not just with eloquent words but with a heart full of genuine compassion. As church leaders, you have likely faced the challenge of bridging diverse communities. There are rewarding moments when love transforms skepticism into belief and turns isolation into fellowship. The call to disciple all nations resonates more deeply when fortified by love's transformative power. In understanding love through 1 John 4:7-21, we see it is not simply a message—it is the very presence of God made tangible. When our outreach is driven by love, our evangelistic efforts become a living testimony that breaks down barriers and nurtures lasting relationships.

LOVE TRANSCENDING BARRIERS

Every community carries untold stories beneath societal labels and stereotypes. For church leaders, understanding these personal narratives is crucial to unlocking love's untapped potential. The parable of the Good Samaritan in Luke 10:25-37 exemplifies how love can transcend deep-seated divisions. In that story, a stranger's compassion heals wounds—both physical and emotional—challenging us to see beyond cultural boundaries. When we embrace a love that is willing to break barriers, we create communities where every individual is recognized for their inherent dignity as a child of God. This radical, transcendent love invites us to reimagine what it means to be a neighbor and to build bridges in our divided world.

INCORPORATING LOVE INTO CHURCH PRACTICES

Incorporating love into the very DNA of church practices requires intentional leadership and a willingness to engage deeply with our communities. Just as the early church thrived on communal living and shared resources in Acts 2:42-47, modern congregations have the opportunity to weave love into every facet of their ministry. This means more than inviting immigrants into our pews—it means actively engaging them in church life and addressing their physical, emotional, and spiritual needs.

For example, consider initiatives such as ESL programs, cultural exchange events, and mentorship initiatives. These practical expressions of love do more than provide aid; they build lasting relationships and create a culture of inclusivity. When church leaders model this inclusive love, it transforms the entire congregation, ensuring that every individual feels valued and empowered to contribute their unique gifts. By integrating these practices, the Church fulfills the Great Commission and creates an environment where love is not just preached but actively practiced.

LIVING A LIFE OF LOVE

Leadership is as much an inward journey as it is an outward expression. True ministry begins with self-examination—a willingness to reflect on how we live out the love of Christ in our everyday lives. James 1:27 calls us to look after orphans and widows and to keep ourselves unstained by the world, challenging each of us to evaluate our personal attitudes toward others.

Ask yourself: How do I show love to those who are different from me? What steps can I take to overcome biases and cultural barriers? The process of personal transformation is not about guilt but about growth—a journey that aligns our hearts with God's vision. When church leaders are open to introspection, they set a powerful example for their congregations. Personal stories of transformation can become seeds that foster an entire culture of love and acceptance within the church.

JESUS' COMMAND OF LOVE

In John 13:34-35, Jesus commands His followers, "A new command I give you: Love one another. As I have loved you, so you must love one another." This command is not just a guideline but the essence of Christian identity. It challenges us to embody a love that breaks down barriers, heals divisions, and brings people together. Jesus' life is the ultimate testament to this command. His interactions—whether dining with outcasts, healing the sick, or engaging with those considered unworthy—demonstrate that love is a powerful, unifying force.

Romans 13:8-10 further underscores that love fulfills the law, binding us together as one body in Christ. For church leaders, this command is both an inspiration and a responsibility. It calls you to lead by example, to nurture an environment where every act of love reflects the grace and mercy of God.

As you reflect on the insights shared in this chapter, remember that love is the Church's most compelling tool for transformation. It is not an abstract ideal but a tangible, living force capable of reshaping societies and fulfilling the call of the Great Commission. When believers embrace the full potential of generous, sacrificial love, they become co-creators in God's kingdom, weaving together a tapestry of unity, inclusion, and hope.

Every act of outreach, every gesture of kindness, and every moment of genuine connection serves as a powerful testimony to God's redemptive love. Imagine a future where churches are universally recognized as sanctuaries of love—places where every individual, regardless of background or circumstance, feels valued, embraced, and empowered.

A CALL TO ACTION

Now, more than ever, the Church must rise to the challenge. The Great Commission compels us to make disciples of all nations, and that mission begins with the way we live out our love daily. I urge you, church leaders and believers alike, to examine your own hearts and communities. Ask yourself: Are we truly living out the command to love one another? Are our ministries designed to break down barriers and embrace every person who walks through our doors?

It's time to take intentional, tangible steps. Begin by integrating initiatives that promote inclusivity—start ESL classes, set up mentorship programs, organize cultural exchange events, and partner with local organizations that support immigrants. Let your church be a beacon of hope, a sanctuary where love is not just a concept but a lived reality.

Remember that every small act of kindness can create ripples that extend far beyond our immediate community. Your leadership is pivotal. When you commit to a ministry infused with love, you not only fulfill the Great Commission but also create a legacy of transformation that can change lives and communities. Let your ministry be a testament to the power of love—a love that knows no boundaries, a love that is radical and all-encompassing.

Today, I challenge you to step out of your comfort zones. Embrace the opportunities before you to be a cheerful giver and a catalyst for change. As you lead with courage and conviction, may you inspire those around you to follow in the footsteps of Christ.

Let every act of love, every gesture of generosity, and every moment of compassion be a proclamation of God's kingdom on earth.

The time for action is now. Stand up, speak out, and let your life be a vibrant witness to the transformative power of love. In doing so, you will not only fulfill your calling but also pave the way for a future where the Church truly reflects the inclusive, radical love of our Savior.

Chapter Six

SHOW MERCY

There is a profound power in mercy—a power that transforms hearts, mends broken communities, and reflects the very nature of God's grace. Mercy is not merely a fleeting emotion or a gentle sentiment; it is an active, life-changing force that calls us to treat others with compassion, justice, and genuine care. In this chapter, we explore the radical theme of mercy, its biblical foundations, and its vital role in fulfilling the Great Commission. Through mercy, the Church is invited to reassess its practices, extend its arms to immigrants and marginalized communities, and model a love that is both inclusive and transformative.

THE BIBLICAL FOUNDATION OF MERCY

Mercy finds its roots deep in Scripture. One of the clearest expressions comes from Leviticus 19:33-34 (NIV): "When a foreigner resides among you in your land, do not mistreat them. The foreigner residing among you must be treated as your native-born. Love them as yourself, for you were foreigners in Egypt. I am the Lord your God."

These verses remind us that mercy is not an optional extra for God's people—it is a divine mandate. The command to treat the foreigner as a native and to love them as oneself is deeply rooted in the historical memory of the Israelites. They were called to remember their own experience of being strangers in a foreign land so that no one would ever be left out or mistreated. This call to mercy is intertwined with the concepts of justice and compassion. The Book of Leviticus, known for its detailed instructions on holy living and sacrifice, sets forth a model that is not solely ritualistic but deeply relational. The guidelines were meant to shape a community that mirrors God's heart—a community where mercy flows like living water and where every person is valued regardless of their background.

Understanding the context of these commands is crucial. The Israelites, having been enslaved in Egypt, knew all too well the pain of neglect and injustice. Thus, the call to extend mercy was a powerful reminder to break the cycle of oppression. This historical perspective is not confined to ancient times; it speaks directly to us today. Just as the Israelites were urged to remember their past and extend love to the stranger, modern believers are invited to do the same in our increasingly diverse society.

UNDERSTANDING MERCY

In our contemporary context, mercy takes on even greater urgency when applied to the immigrant experience. Immigrants, like every human being, are created in the image of God. Yet, they frequently face injustice, discrimination, and neglect. When we withhold mercy, we not only fail to honor God's command but also miss a critical opportunity to transform lives and heal communities.

Believers are called to view the world through the lens of Scripture rather than solely through personal experience or societal norms. Too often, the Church risks viewing others only through a narrow perspective, forgetting that every individual reflects the image of God. The mandate in Leviticus challenges us to step outside our comfort zones and recognize the inherent dignity of every immigrant. Mercy means actively confronting and dismantling the structures of injustice—whether they be cultural biases, flawed policies, or even unintentional neglect within our own church communities.

As church leaders, we must advocate for immigrants not only through words but also through decisive actions. This includes providing practical support such as legal aid, language classes, and community resources, as well as extending spiritual guidance. Mercy demands that we see immigrants as whole persons, deserving of our compassion and care and that we actively work to build communities where they are fully integrated and embraced.

MERCY IN ACTION: BIBLICAL EXAMPLES

Biblical narratives offer profound examples of mercy in action. Consider the example of Abraham in Genesis 18:1-8. Abraham welcomed three visitors into his tent with extraordinary generosity and mercy, offering them food, rest, and comfort— even though he did not initially know their true identity. His actions are a powerful model of how we should treat every guest. Abraham's willingness to care for the stranger speaks volumes about the heart of mercy—a heart that looks beyond the immediate and reaches for something eternal.

Similarly, the laws in Leviticus 19:33-34 serve as a constant reminder that mercy is at the core of God's expectations for His people. The command to "love them as yourself" is not merely a call for kindness but a radical reorientation of our attitudes toward others. It calls us to remember our own history as foreigners so that we can extend the same mercy we once received.

In the New Testament, Jesus amplifies this message. His parables, such as that of the Good Samaritan in Luke 10:25-37, illustrate that mercy is not an optional extra—it is essential to the Christian life. In this parable, the Samaritan's compassionate act towards a wounded stranger challenges us to overcome deep-seated cultural and racial divides. Jesus' teaching in Matthew 25:35-40 reinforces this truth by declaring that every act of mercy toward the least among us is, in effect, an act of mercy toward Him.

These biblical narratives provide a powerful blueprint for us. They remind us that mercy is multifaceted: it involves meeting physical needs, offering emotional support, and extending spiritual guidance. Mercy is a holistic approach to care—a calling that the Church is invited to embody in every aspect of its ministry.

MERCY AND THE GREAT COMMISSION

The Great Commission calls us to make disciples of all nations, and mercy is an essential component of this mission. When the Church embraces mercy, it creates an environment in which the Gospel can truly flourish. Acts of mercy break down the barriers that separate people, paving the way for deep, transformative relationships. Imagine a church that not only preaches the Gospel but also actively demonstrates it through acts of compassion. When we extend mercy, we create opportunities for evangelism that go beyond words. We become living testaments to God's grace, showing the world that His love is not confined to Sunday services but is evident in every act of kindness, every supportive gesture, and every moment of genuine care.

By integrating mercy into our ministries, we reframe the Great Commission. It becomes not merely a task to be completed through preaching and teaching but a holistic mission that encompasses the physical, emotional, and spiritual well-being of every person. Mercy, therefore, becomes the engine that drives our outreach, transforming our ministry into a force for lasting change.

PRACTICAL STEPS FOR EMBRACING MERCY

To live out the radical theme of mercy, the Church must implement practical strategies that are both reflective and action-oriented. Here are some concrete steps to help integrate mercy into every facet of ministry:

- **Develop Comprehensive Outreach Programs:** Create initiatives that specifically address the needs of immigrant communities—food and clothing drives, health clinics, and temporary shelter programs. Ensure these programs are designed with empathy and accessibility in mind. By addressing immediate needs, the Church demonstrates tangible mercy and lays the groundwork for deeper spiritual engagement.

- **Implement Educational Workshops and Seminars:** Offer classes on legal rights, financial literacy, and language acquisition. These workshops empower immigrants by equipping them with the knowledge and skills necessary to navigate their new environment. Education is an act of mercy that not only transforms lives but also fosters self-reliance and community integration.

- **Create Safe Spaces for Dialogue:** Establish forums or support groups where immigrants can share their experiences, challenges, and hopes. Facilitated discussions allow both immigrants and long-time members to learn from each other, promoting mutual understanding and healing. Such safe spaces help break down isolation and build a sense of belonging.

- **Advocate for Just Policies:** Partner with local organizations to provide legal aid and to advocate for humane immigration policies. When the Church speaks out against injustice and supports policies that protect the vulnerable, it acts as a prophetic voice in society—one that embodies mercy and defends human dignity.

- **Train Church Leaders and Members:** Organize training sessions and workshops on cultural sensitivity and the importance of mercy in ministry. Encourage leaders to examine their own biases and develop strategies to create more inclusive environments. When the Church invests in the personal and spiritual growth of its members, it fosters a culture where mercy is deeply ingrained in every interaction.

- **Celebrate Diversity Through Community Events:** Host

multicultural festivals, heritage nights, and community meals that celebrate the rich diversity of God's creation. These events serve as joyful expressions of mercy, providing opportunities for immigrants to share their culture and for the congregation to learn and grow together. Celebrating diversity reinforces that every person is a valuable part of the Church's mosaic.

- **Incorporate Mercy into Worship and Teaching:** Ensure that sermons, Bible studies, and small group discussions frequently address the theme of mercy. Use Scriptures such as Leviticus 19:33-34 and the parable of the Good Samaritan to illustrate how God's mercy should inform our attitudes and actions. A regular emphasis on mercy in teaching reinforces its importance as a core value of the Church.

Each of these steps is designed to not only meet immediate needs but also to build lasting relationships. When mercy is practiced intentionally, it creates ripples that transform lives and entire communities. The Church, by investing in these practical initiatives, becomes a sanctuary where every individual feels valued, supported, and empowered.

INTERNAL TRANSFORMATION: A HEART OF MERCY

For mercy to permeate every action, there must be an internal transformation within the Church—a change of heart that then radiates outward in every interaction. This internal shift is critical, as it sets the tone for how the community engages with the world.

Cultural awareness and sensitivity are essential components of this transformation. As the Church seeks to understand the diverse backgrounds of immigrants, it must engage in ongoing education and self-reflection. Workshops, training sessions, and facilitated dialogues can help congregants identify and overcome their biases, enabling them to interact with others more empathetically and respectfully.

This process is not solely about acquiring knowledge—it is about a change of heart. When church members begin to see immigrants as fellow bearers of God's image, their willingness to extend mercy grows naturally. Personal stories of transformation, shared within the community, serve as powerful reminders of how acts of mercy can change lives. Reflect on your own journey: How has a single act of kindness or a generous gesture altered your perspective? These experiences are the seeds of internal change that eventually lead to a broader culture of mercy within the Church.

As each individual undergoes this inward transformation, it radiates outward, creating a Church that not only serves others but embodies the true spirit of the Gospel. This personal growth, nurtured by a commitment to mercy, ultimately contributes to a unified, compassionate community that reflects the love of Christ in every action.

JESUS' COMMAND TO LOVE AND SHOW MERCY

In John 13:34-35, Jesus commands His disciples, "A new command I give you: Love one another. As I have loved you, so you must love one another." This command is not merely about warm feelings—it is about active, selfless mercy that transforms lives. Jesus' ministry was characterized by radical acts of mercy: He healed the sick, fed the hungry, and embraced those whom society had cast aside. His example challenges us to do the same.

Romans 13:8-10 reinforces that love is the fulfillment of the law. It calls us to break down all barriers and live in a manner that reflects God's mercy. For church leaders, this command is both an inspiration and a mandate. It calls you to examine your ministry and ensure that every program, every outreach, and every interaction is steeped in the mercy of Christ. When your life and leadership reflect this divine mandate, you set an example that transforms your community and radiates God's love to the world.

A UNIFIED CALL TO ACTION

Now, as we conclude this chapter on mercy, the time for action is clear. Mercy is not an abstract concept to be admired from afar—it is a powerful, practical force that must be lived out daily. I invite you, whether you are a church leader or a devoted believer, to take these reflections to heart and put them into action.

Evaluate your ministry: Are you actively creating environments where mercy is evident? Do your outreach programs, educational initiatives, and community events reflect a deep, transformative mercy that reaches those in need? Consider partnering with local organizations to advocate for fair and humane policies, to support legal aid, or to offer services that empower immigrants. Embrace the call to internal transformation, letting your personal journey be marked by a willingness to see every individual as God sees them—a person deserving of mercy, respect, and love. The time to act is now. Step out of your comfort zone and challenge yourself to embody the radical mercy that Jesus demonstrated. Your every act of kindness, every outreach effort, and every moment of compassionate engagement is a declaration that, in God's eyes, no one is undeserving of mercy. Let your life and ministry become living testimonies to the transformative power of mercy—a mercy that breaks down barriers unites communities and builds the Kingdom of God on earth.

May your ministry be a beacon of hope—a sanctuary where mercy flows freely, where every heart is embraced, and where the redemptive power of God's love is evident in every action. Embrace this divine call with courage and conviction, knowing that every step you take in mercy is a step toward fulfilling the Great Commission and creating a community that reflects the inclusive, boundless love of our Savior.

Step out boldly and be the living example of mercy that this world so desperately needs. Your journey of mercy can transform lives, heal wounds, and inspire others to join in building a Church that is truly a home for all.

Chapter Seven

A HOME AWAY FROM HOME

The Church is meant to be more than just a building or a gathering—it is a community, a place of belonging where every individual can find refuge, purpose, and a sense of identity. In today's world, where many immigrants feel isolated or marginalized, the call for the Church to be a "home away from home" becomes ever more vital. This chapter explores the radical theme of the Church as a community and a place of belonging, highlighting how this principle is not only foundational to the Great Commission but also essential for building bridges in our diverse society.

Imagine a place where, regardless of background or circumstance, every person is welcomed with open arms, where the Church becomes a sanctuary that reflects the inclusive love of God. In such a community, the unfamiliar becomes familiar, and strangers are embraced as family. This is the heart of radical hospitality—a home where all who enter are seen, valued, and loved.

THE CHURCH: A PLACE OF BELONGING

Referring back to Montañez's insights, the notion of the Church as a community and a place of belonging is perhaps the final, yet most powerful, tenet of radical hospitality. Scripture reminds us of this calling in Matthew 25:35 (NIV): "For I was hungry, and you gave me something to eat, I was thirsty, and you gave me something to drink, I was a stranger, and you invited me in, I needed clothes, and you clothed me, I was sick, and you looked after me, I was in prison, and you came to visit me."

These words speak to the transformative potential of the Church when it becomes a living embodiment of God's love and care. The Church is called to be a place where every need is met—not just physical needs, but emotional and spiritual ones as well. It is in this environment that individuals find hope, healing, and a renewed sense of belonging.

Historically, the Church has been both a refuge and a rallying point for those who have felt estranged or abandoned by society. When the early believers gathered, they formed communities that broke down cultural and social barriers. They shared meals, supported one another, and created a sense of unity that transcended their differences. Today, we face similar challenges. In a society that often isolates immigrants and treats them as outsiders, the Church must rise to the occasion and redefine what it means to be a family in Christ.

In our modern context, the Church's failure to create a genuine home for immigrants is not just a missed opportunity for evangelism—it is a failure to live out the heart of the Gospel. When immigrants are treated as perpetual outsiders, it sends a message that the love of Christ is limited. But God's love is boundless. Every person, regardless of their origin, is created in the image of God (Genesis 1:27) and is, therefore, worthy of belonging and dignity.

THE BIBLICAL MANDATE FOR BELONGING

The Bible consistently emphasizes that all people belong to God's kingdom. In addition to Matthew 25:35, we see this call echoed in the parable of the Good Samaritan found in Luke 10:25-37. This parable tells the story of a Samaritan who, despite the deep-seated enmity between his people and the Jews, stops to help a wounded stranger. The Samaritan's actions illustrate that true compassion transcends ethnic, cultural, and social divisions. His willingness to care for someone society deemed an enemy reminds us that the Church is called to break down barriers and to offer a welcoming embrace to all.

Furthermore, in Acts 2:44-47, the early Church is depicted as a community where believers shared everything in common. They broke bread in their homes, supported one another's needs, and experienced a profound sense of unity. This historical example challenges us to rethink our modern church communities. Are we truly living out this radical inclusivity? Are we creating spaces where every person, especially immigrants, feels at home?

The biblical mandate for belonging is clear: we are to love our neighbors as ourselves. This means that the Church must look beyond superficial differences and embrace each person with the same compassion and generosity that God has shown us. When we do this, we not only fulfill the Great Commission but also become a tangible representation of God's kingdom on earth.

CREATING A HOME AWAY FROM HOME

Despite this clear mandate, many churches struggle to create environments that feel truly inclusive. Cultural barriers, socioeconomic divisions, and historical prejudices can all conspire to leave immigrants feeling like perpetual outsiders. In some cases, the very structures of ministry are designed with only one cultural narrative in mind, often ignoring the rich diversity of God's people.

For instance, traditional church programs might cater primarily to a homogeneous group, leaving immigrants without a sense of belonging. When the Church views its membership through a narrow lens, it inadvertently reinforces divisions rather than breaking them down. This challenge is compounded by broader societal attitudes that often devalue immigrant contributions, creating an environment where marginalized voices are silenced.

Moreover, logistical challenges—such as language barriers and unfamiliarity with cultural norms—can make it difficult for immigrants to fully participate in church life. When these barriers are left unaddressed, they not only hinder spiritual growth but also prevent the Church from being the inclusive, transformative community it is called to be.

Yet, these challenges are not insurmountable. Recognizing these obstacles is the first step toward overcoming them. By acknowledging the unique struggles faced by immigrants, the Church can begin to implement strategies that foster true belonging.

PRACTICAL STRATEGIES FOR FOSTERING BELONGING

In order to be a home away from home, the Church must adopt practical strategies that create a welcoming environment for immigrants. Drawing from both biblical principles and contemporary ministry practices, here are several actionable suggestions:

Culturally Responsive Worship: Develop worship services that reflect the diversity of your congregation. This might include incorporating multiple languages in hymns and prayers, or celebrating different cultural expressions of worship. A culturally responsive service sends a powerful message: every member's background is valued and honored.

Inclusive Communication: Ensure that all church communications—bulletins, websites, and announcements—are accessible to non-native English speakers. Consider offering translated materials or utilizing visual media to convey key messages. When communication is inclusive, it helps immigrants feel connected and informed.

1. **Intercultural Small Groups:** Establish small groups that intentionally bring together individuals from different cultural backgrounds. These groups can serve as safe spaces for sharing personal stories, discussing faith, and building genuine relationships. Intercultural groups encourage mutual understanding and foster a sense of unity within the diverse body of the church.

2. **Welcome Teams and Mentorship Programs:** Create dedicated welcome teams tasked with reaching out to new immigrants. These teams can provide practical assistance—

such as guidance on local customs, language support, and information about church services—and offer personal mentorship. This hands-on approach ensures that every newcomer feels seen and cared for from the moment they step through the door.

3. **Community Engagement and Outreach:** Partner with local immigrant organizations and community centers to host events that celebrate cultural diversity. Whether it's a multicultural festival, a community meal, or a language exchange program, these events can build bridges between the church and the broader community, demonstrating that the Church is a vibrant, inclusive family.

4. **Educational Workshops:** Offer workshops that educate the congregation about immigrant cultures and the challenges they face. These sessions can address topics like cultural sensitivity, historical immigration struggles, and practical ways to support newcomers. Knowledge fosters empathy, and understanding the immigrant experience is key to building a more inclusive church environment.

5. **Advocacy for Immigrant Rights:** The Church can also serve as a prophetic voice by advocating for fair and compassionate immigration policies. This might include hosting forums on immigration issues, partnering with advocacy groups, or even writing letters to local government officials. Such actions not only support immigrants on a systemic level but also demonstrate the Church's commitment to justice.

6. **Celebratory Events:** Host regular events that celebrate the diversity within your congregation. Whether through potlucks, cultural nights, or shared holiday celebrations,

these gatherings offer opportunities for fellowship and joy. They create a space where differences are celebrated, and every member feels part of a larger family.

By integrating these strategies, the Church can begin to break down the barriers that leave immigrants feeling isolated. Each initiative is an opportunity to live out the biblical mandate of belonging, ensuring that every individual is welcomed, valued, and equipped to contribute to the community's life and mission.

CULTIVATING A HEART OF BELONGING

For the Church to truly be a home away from home, there must be an internal transformation that starts with every individual. This transformation begins with a willingness to examine personal biases and embrace a broader, more inclusive vision of what it means to be a community.

Leaders and members alike must engage in honest self-reflection—asking tough questions about how they view and treat others. This introspection is not meant to induce guilt but to foster growth. When we see immigrants not as outsiders but as fellow bearers of God's image, our actions naturally reflect a deeper, more genuine love.

Training sessions, workshops, and small group discussions can facilitate this internal transformation. By sharing personal testimonies of how generosity and inclusion have transformed lives, church members can inspire one another to embrace a culture of belonging. When internal change occurs, it radiates outward, reshaping the entire church environment into one that truly reflects the kingdom of God.

A CALL TO ACTION

The challenge before the Church is clear: Will we continue to allow immigrants to remain on the fringes, or will we transform our communities into true homes where every individual feels welcomed and valued? The call to create a "home away from home" is not an optional extra—it is central to our mission and our identity as followers of Christ.

I urge you, church leaders and members alike, to take these insights to heart and put them into action. Evaluate your current ministry practices: Are you intentionally creating spaces where immigrants can experience genuine belonging? If not, consider how you can integrate the practical strategies outlined above—culturally responsive worship, inclusive communication, intercultural small groups, dedicated welcome teams, community outreach, educational workshops, advocacy, and celebratory events.

Each act of intentional inclusion and every effort to break down cultural barriers is a step toward fulfilling the Great Commission. Remember, every time you extend a warm welcome, every time you listen to someone's story, and every time you celebrate cultural diversity, you are building a community that mirrors the unconditional love of Christ.

Now is the time for transformation. Step out of your comfort zones and commit to creating a church environment where all feel at home. Let your ministry be a vibrant tapestry woven from diverse threads—a place where every immigrant finds not just acceptance but true belonging. Your leadership can spark a ripple effect that transforms lives, heals divisions, and paves the way for a more unified, compassionate community.

As you leave this chapter, take with you the conviction that the Church is called to be a refuge—a home where love is the currency and every individual is cherished. Embrace this divine mandate with courage and dedication. Your efforts in fostering a community of belonging are not only fulfilling the Great Commission but are also a powerful testimony of God's boundless love and mercy.

May you be inspired to create a sanctuary of hope—a place where every heart finds its home, every voice is heard, and every life is transformed by the power of belonging. Let your actions, your words, and your leadership speak of a Church that truly is a home away from home, where love, compassion, and unity reign supreme.

Thoughts

Chapter Eight

FINAL WORDS FROM THE AUTHOR

A s I sit down to write these final words, I am filled with a profound sense of gratitude and determination. The journey of writing this book has been one of deep reflection and honest self-examination—a journey that has brought me face-to-face with the challenges, triumphs, and opportunities inherent in fulfilling the Great Commission right here at home. "Disciples of All Nations: Making the Great Commission Our Daily Mission" is more than a title; it is a clarion call—a vision and roadmap for every believer who longs to see God's kingdom flourish through the transformation of lives.

This book has been my heart laid bare, a testament to a life shaped by both the blessings and the struggles of being part of a multicultural community. Growing up as a child of immigrant parents, I have experienced both the pain of feeling like an outsider and the profound impact of being embraced by genuine love. Throughout these pages, I have explored the themes of compassion, generosity, love, mercy, and belonging—not as abstract concepts but as vital, practical elements of our mission as followers of Christ.

Instead of merely recapping each chapter, I want to share with you how these themes have personally transformed my perspective and how they continue to shape my journey. In my early years, I often felt the sting of isolation—my accent, my customs, and my heritage marked me as different. I encountered barriers in every facet of life, from the military to the church, where I longed for acceptance and genuine connection. These experiences ignited within me a passion for reconciliation—a longing to see the Church become a true sanctuary for all people, especially those who are too often overlooked.

My journey of self-discovery led me to pursue doctoral research at Huntsville Bible College, where I delved deeply into the Church's role in reaching out to immigrants. It was during that time that one word kept echoing in my prayers: RECONCILIATION. I came to see that our ministry efforts often fall short because we fail to intentionally embrace those who are different from us. The insights I gained were both painful and illuminating. I realized that the Church, as it stands in many communities, is missing an essential piece of its mission—a vibrant, inclusive love that not only preaches the Gospel but lives it out through radical hospitality, generous giving, and merciful care.

Reflecting on these insights, I am reminded that the call of the Great Commission is not reserved for a select few. It is for every one of us. It is not enough to simply attend church on Sundays or offer a polite smile; we must actively engage, reaching out to our neighbors and extending the love of Christ in tangible ways. I have seen firsthand the transformative power of a warm welcome, the healing force of a kind word, and the deep connection that forms when we share our lives with those who are different. These experiences have taught me that when we truly open our hearts, barriers break down, and communities are transformed.

Each chapter of this book has built upon these truths. In exploring the biblical mandate of the Great Commission, we discovered that Jesus calls us to step beyond our comfort zones and reach out to all nations. In examining compassion and inclusivity, we learned that true ministry requires us to break down cultural barriers and embrace diversity as a gift from God. The discussions on radical hospitality showed us that the Church is not merely a building but a living community—a home where every person is welcomed. Our exploration of generosity revealed that when we give freely, we become channels of God's transformative power. Our reflection on mercy underscored the need to care for the vulnerable, reminding us that every act of kindness is a reflection of God's redemptive love.

Yet, these themes are not merely academic or theoretical. They are the very lifeblood of the Gospel, the principles that have sustained me through times of struggle and uncertainty. They are the qualities I see in the eyes of those who have touched my life—the immigrant who found solace in a simple act of kindness, the stranger who became a friend through a shared meal, the community that rose together in mutual support and understanding. These are the moments that remind me that our mission is both urgent and eternal.

I want to speak directly to you, dear reader—whether you are a church leader, a congregant, or someone seeking to understand your place in God's unfolding story. Your journey has led you here because you have a heart that desires change, a heart that is ready to step into a role that is as challenging as it is rewarding. I ask you to take a moment to reflect on the times you have felt truly seen, welcomed, and loved. Those moments are not coincidences; they are expressions of God's grace at work in our lives. Now, imagine if every believer, every church, made it their daily mission to extend that same grace to others—especially to those who feel forgotten or unwelcome.

The call of the Great Commission is clear: go and make disciples of all nations. But how can we do this if our churches are not places of genuine belonging? How can we reach a hurting world if we ourselves are not living in the fullness of God's love and mercy? The answer lies in radical hospitality—a willingness to tear down the walls that separate us, embrace our differences, and build communities that mirror the inclusive, boundless love of our Savior.

I challenge you to examine your own church's practices. Look at your outreach programs, your worship services, and your daily interactions with newcomers. Ask yourself: Are we building bridges, or are we inadvertently reinforcing divisions? Are we actively making space for every individual, or are we leaving some on the fringes? Every small step you take toward embracing radical hospitality can have a profound impact. It could be as simple as greeting someone in their native language or as transformative as creating a mentorship program that pairs long-time members with new immigrants. These are the building blocks of a community where the Gospel is not only preached but lived out authentically.

I also urge you to look inward. The journey of radical hospitality begins with personal transformation—a willingness to confront your own biases and to open your heart to a broader, more inclusive vision. Remember that you, too, were once a stranger in need of grace. Let the memories of times when you experienced God's mercy inspire you to extend that same mercy to others. It is in our vulnerability and willingness to change that true community is born.

As I reflect on the legacy I hope to leave, I envision a future where every church is truly a home away from home—a sanctuary where every immigrant, every sojourner, and every stranger finds not just acceptance but belonging. I dream of communities united by love and built on the foundation of the Gospel—a legacy of radical hospitality that transforms lives, heals wounds, and brings us closer to the Kingdom of God.

My prayer is that the insights in this book will ignite a passion for change in your heart. Let the lessons of compassion, generosity, mercy, and inclusion guide your every step. Allow these truths to reshape your ministry and your life so that you become a beacon of hope and a living testimony to the transformative power of the Gospel.

Now is the time to act. I call upon you, dear reader, to step out in faith and embrace the mission set before us. Evaluate your church's culture, reflect on your personal journey, and consider how you can be a catalyst for change. Whether you choose to launch a new ministry, enhance existing programs, or simply alter the way you interact with your neighbors, know that every act of love has the power to create lasting ripples in the world.

Imagine a future where the Church is universally recognized as a home away from home—a sanctuary where every heart finds nourishment, every voice is heard, and every life is transformed by the power of belonging. This is not an unattainable dream; it is a vision rooted in the truth of Scripture and the promise of God's unending grace. As disciples of all nations, we are called to turn this vision into reality. It begins with each one of us—our willingness to love, to serve, and to make room for those who have been marginalized.

I challenge you to let your actions speak louder than words. Let your ministry be characterized by bold, compassionate outreach. Build bridges where there are walls; extend kindness where there is indifference; and offer hope where there is despair. Your leadership, your commitment to living out the Gospel, and your readiness to embrace every person with open arms will shape the future of the Church and impact countless lives.

These final words are not the end of our journey but a new beginning—a call to transform our communities and fulfill the Great Commission with every breath we take. May you be inspired to create a legacy of radical hospitality that echoes the love of Christ for generations to come.

This is our mission. This is our calling. And it begins with you.

ABOUT THE AUTHOR

D r. Elouise P. Bradsher has served as a member of the National Coalition of 100 Black Women since 2019. She is a member and board member of the League of Women Voters of Tennessee Valley (LWVTV). She also serves as the Logistics Management Specialist for the Logistics Data Analysis Center (LDAC) Installation Readiness Office. Previously, she served on active duty as an Automated Logistical Specialist (92A) in the United States Army from 1981 to 2005. Dr. Bradsher retired after 24 years of service in the United States Army with multiple deployments, including to Germany, Kosovo, and Korea.

Dr. Bradsher served as a Senior Logistics Analyst for LogiCore Corporation from 2006 to 2019. She was honored for her outstanding achievement in attaining the Army Demonstrated Master Logistician Designation by The International Society of Logistics and The Army Logistics University on March 5, 2017.

Additionally, for her outstanding professional achievements and contributions while serving as a Senior Logistics Analyst at the Army Materiel Command through LogiCore Corporation, Dr. Bradsher was awarded the President's Award for Employee of the Quarter on December 7, 2017.

In 2019, Dr. Bradsher served as a Senior Logistics Analyst in HQ Army Materiel Command (AMC) Readiness Division. She oversaw Army readiness data from a variety of sources and compiled them into coherent, informative reports for AMC and the Army's senior leaders. Her support enabled the Commanding General (CG) of AMC to address ARNG readiness issues and AMC's efforts to support the ARNG. Her systematic approach enabled the Deputy Commanding General (DCG) to discuss ongoing AMC efforts in support of the respective Brigade Combat Teams (BCTs). Dr. Bradsher was awarded the LogiCore Corporation Certificate of Excellence for her diligence and dedication, which reflect great credit upon her and the AMC Readiness Team.

Dr. Bradsher is a proud member of the Army Acquisition Corps Workforce. Her education includes DAWIA Acquisition Professional Certification (Level III in Life Cycle Logistics and Level I in Program Management), as well as completion of the Civilian Education System (CES) Foundation, Intermediate Courses, and Advanced Course Phase I.

Her awards and decorations include the Commander's Award for Civilian Service (25 years), the Meritorious Service Medal, Army Commendation Medal, Army Achievement Medal, Army Good Conduct Medal, National Defense Service Medal, Korean Defense Service Medal, Global War on Terrorism Service Medal,

Army Service Ribbon, Non-Commissioned Officer's Professional Development Ribbon, and the Army Demonstrated Master Logistician Award Designation by SOLE – The International Society of Logistics. Dr. Bradsher is also a recipient of the Honorable Order of Saint Martin from the United States Army Association of Quartermasters.

Dr. Bradsher has three children—one son and two daughters— and six grandchildren. She holds a Bachelor of Science in Management Studies/Administration with Honors from Excelsior College, a Master of Arts in Education with Distinction, Summa Cum Laude, from Touro University International, and a Doctor of Ministry in Biblical Leadership from Huntsville Bible College, graduating with high honors—Summa Cum Laude.

CONNECT WITH THE AUTHOR

Thank you for reading *Disciples of All Nations*. Follow Dr. Elouise P. Griffith-Bradsher on social media to stay updated on her ministry work.

FACEBOOK   Elouise Bradsher

INSTAGRAM   @elouisepbradsher

www.ingramcontent.com/pod-product-compliance
Lightning Source LLC
Chambersburg PA
CBHW031928080426
42734CB00007B/601